tanoshii
wagashi

tanoshii
wagashi

little bites of japanese delights

Yamashita Masataka

mc Marshall Cavendish
Cuisine

Chef Yamashita would like to thank Mr Nobuaki Hirohashi for the loan of the beautiful plates used during the photography session, and Mr Kiyotaka Imanishi for supplying the lovely sake for the jelly recipe in this book.

Editor: Lydia Leong
Designer: Adithi Khandadi
Photographer: Hongde Photography

Other Marshall Cavendish Offices:
Marshall Cavendish Corporation. 99 White Plains Road, Tarrytown NY 10591-9001, USA • Marshall Cavendish International (Thailand) Co Ltd. 253 Asoke, 12th Flr, Sukhumvit 21 Road, Klongtoey Nua, Wattana, Bangkok 10110, Thailand • Marshall Cavendish (Malaysia) Sdn Bhd, Times Subang, Lot 46, Subang Hi-Tech Industrial Park, Batu Tiga, 40000 Shah Alam, Selangor Darul Ehsan, Malaysia

Marshall Cavendish is a trademark of Times Publishing Limited

National Library Board, Singapore Cataloguing-in-Publication Data

Yamashita, Masataka, author.
Tanoshii wagashi : little bites of Japanese delights / Yamashita Masataka. – Singapore : Marshall Cavendish Cuisine, 2014
pages cm
ISBN : 978-981-4516-49-5 (paperback)

1. Confectionery ~ Japan. 2. Cooking, Japanese. 3. Cookbooks. I. Title.

TX783
641.8530952 -- dc23 OCN889992525

Printed in Singapore by Markono Print Media Pte Ltd

DEDICATION

To my beloved Ami.
Thanks for always being by
my side through thick and thin
—we finally have our very own
shop in Singapore!

CONTENTS

MODERN ADAPTATIONS

PACKAGING IDEAS 100
PAIRING WAGASHI WITH DRINKS 102
GLOSSARY 106
WEIGHTS & MEASURES 111

ACKNOWLEDGEMENTS

I would like to thank the following people for making this book possible:

My friend, Lincoln Tan, for helping me translate the recipes
and communicating with the various parties involved
in spite of his busy work schedule as a lawyer.

My friend, Linh Luong, who is like a daughter to me,
for helping me write the recipes and the introduction.

My editor, Lydia Leong, for working with me to produce this second book,
and for relentlessly reminding me and helping me to keep to the deadline.
It was a great pleasure working with her once again.

The photographer, Liu Hongde, for his tiresome efforts and the designer,
Adithi Khandadai, for her creative efforts.
Producing this book would not have been as much fun without them.

My wonderful team at Chef Yamashita who went out of their way and
contributed so much to the production of this book.

Thank you.

I CAREFULLY SELECTED THE RECIPES
TO MAKE SURE EACH ONE
IS EASY TO FOLLOW.

INTRODUCTION

When we meet someone again or for the first time, we often say, "Hello". But let me start by saying "Thank you" for bringing home with you my second book, *Tanoshii Wagashi*. The encouragement and support I received for my first book, *Tanoshii*, inspired me so much that I felt compelled to continue sharing with you the beauty and joy of making sweets and desserts.

As a chef from Nara, Japan, I was professionally trained in Japanese baking styles. The techniques I learned fascinated me. All these years, creating beautiful, delicious cakes and sweets for others has been my greatest passion. I believe I can bring much happiness to those around me through the pastries that I make. And I believe you can do the same.

Like *Tanoshii*, my first cookbook, I hope this book will also enable you to create wonderful, tasty sweets in your own home. While my first book focuses on popular French-style pastries, this time around, I would like to introduce to you to a delightful part of the Japanese culture.

Wagashi refers to traditional Japanese sweets. In this book, I have specially come up with a selection of traditional and modern Japanese-style sweets, which I hope you will enjoy. I always believe that with sufficient guidance, baking can be a fun and enjoyable experience for everyone. That is why during the months of putting together this book, I carefully selected the recipes to make sure each one is easy to follow. Even if you are a novice in the kitchen, the techniques involved are friendly and manageable.

The ingredients used in this book are not hard to find and are available at local supermarkets and baking supply stores in Singapore. The recipes also do not require special equipment—simple pots, bowls, baking trays, spoons, spatulas and a whisk—will be enough to create these Japanese treats with fun and ease.

In Japan, *wagashi* is often enjoyed with tea, so to complete your enjoyment of these treats, I have included recommendations for pairing different beverages with the different *wagashi*. In addition to this, there is also a section filled with packaging and wrapping ideas, so you can share your *wagashi* with family and friends.

With this new cookbook in your hands, it is now time to try out the recipes! I encourage you to have fun while doing so and not to worry if things don't work out the first time. Familiarise yourself with the recipe and try again.

I am deeply grateful that you are buying my book, but the greater joy comes when I know you have tried out my suggestions and succeeded in making what you like. I am sure it will also bring your loved ones much happiness to try what you have created or join you in the process of making *wagashi*.

I wish you a joyful time filled with beautiful *wagashi* that you will now be able to create by yourself in your own kitchen.

Chef Yamashita Masataka

I WISH YOU A JOYFUL TIME
FILLED WITH
BEAUTIFUL WAGASHI

JAPANESE
BEAN PASTES

SHIRO-AN
(WHITE BEAN PASTE)

— makes about 300 g —

Canned butter beans 240 g

Japanese custard sugar 95 g

1. Drain the butter beans and rinse lightly with water. Place into a basin of water and leave to soak overnight to remove some of the saltiness.

2. Drain the soaked beans. Peel off and discard the thin skin.

3. Place the skinned beans into a food processor and blend into a smooth purée.

4. Transfer the purée to a saucepan. Add the sugar and cook over medium heat, stirring constantly with a spatula until the purée leaves the sides of the saucepan. Test if the mixture is ready by lifting it with the spatula. It should hang down and form a smooth triangular shape. If it does not, continue to stir over medium heat and test again.

5. Store *shiro-an* in small portions and use as needed. *Shiro-an* will keep for 2–3 days in the refrigerator or up to 1 week in the freezer.

TSUBU-AN
(WHOLE RED BEAN PASTE)

— makes about 450 g —

Azuki **(red beans)** 300 g, soaked
 overnight

Water as needed

Japanese custard sugar 260 g

Salt a pinch

1. Drain the beans and place into a 20-cm wide pot with
   600 ml water. Bring to the boil over high heat. When the
   water is boiling, add 200 ml cold water to the pot. Let the
   water return to the boil, then remove from heat. Drain and
   rinse the beans.

2. Return the beans to the pot and add 850 ml water. Bring
   to the boil over high heat. When the water is boiling, lower
   the heat and simmer for 40–60 minutes until the beans are
   tender. Add more water if necessary.

3. Drain the beans and return to the pot. Place over low heat.
   Add half the sugar and stir constantly with a spatula until
   the sugar is melted.

4. Add the remaining sugar and salt and continue stirring until
   the beans leave the sides of the pot. Test if the paste is
   ready by lifting the paste with the spatula. It should hang
   down and form a triangular shape. Continue cooking for
   another few minutes if necessary.

5. Store *tsubu-an* in small portions and use as needed.
   Tsubu-an will keep for 2–3 days in the refrigerator or
   up to 1 week in the freezer.

KOSHI-AN
(FINE RED BEAN PASTE)

— makes about 300 g —

Azuki **(red beans)** 250 g, soaked overnight and drained

Water as needed

Japanese custard sugar 240 g

Salt ¼ tsp

1. Place the beans in a pot and cover with water. Bring to the boil over medium heat. When the water is boiling, add 50 ml cold water to the pot. Let the water return to the boil, then remove from heat. Drain and rinse the beans.

2. Repeat the above process of boiling the beans another two times. When boiling the beans for the third time, lower the heat and let simmer for about an hour. Add more water gradually as it boils down, keeping the beans submerged.

3. Test if the beans are ready by pressing a bean between your fingers. It should be soft enough to be easily crushed. Continue to simmer if the beans are still not soft enough.

4. Press the beans through a coarse sieve into a mixing bowl half-filled with water. Discard the skins. Let the mixture sit until the water separates from the paste. Using a small ladle, gently strain off and discard the water.

5. Transfer the paste to a bowl lined with a clean cotton cloth. Twist the cloth to squeeze out all the water from the paste.

6. Place the paste in a pot over low heat. Add half the sugar and mix until the sugar is melted. Add the remaining sugar and salt.

7. Stir constantly until the sugar is melted and the paste leaves the sides of the pot. Test if the paste is ready by lifting with the spatula. It should hang down and form a sticky triangular shape. If it does not, continue to stir over low heat for another few minutes and test again.

8. Transfer the paste to an aluminium tray and let cool in the refrigerator.

9. Store *koshi-an* in small portions and use as needed. *Koshi-an* will keep for 2–3 days in the refrigerator or up to 1 week in the freezer.

TRADITIONAL WAGASHI

DORAYAKI
(PANCAKES WITH RED BEAN PASTE)

— makes about 4 dorayaki —

Eggs 2, medium

Japanese custard sugar 120 g

Honey 15 g

Baking powder ¼ tsp

Water 60 ml

Pastry flour 130 g, sifted

Salad oil as needed

Koshi-an **(page 22)** 180–200 g, divided into 8 equal portions and rolled into balls

---

Tip For evenly coloured and round pancakes, let the batter fall from the spoon into the pan from a single point, and do not swirl the pan. See photo 3.

---

1. Crack the eggs into a large bowl and whisk lightly. Add the sugar and whisk until the mixture is pale. Add the honey and whisk again.

2. Mix the baking powder with the water and add to the bowl.

3. Add the pastry flour, making sure there are no lumps.

4. Heat a frying pan to 180–200°C and brush with oil. Lower the heat and test if the pan is at the right temperature by dropping a small drop of batter (about 1.5 cm diameter) into the pan. When the batter starts to bubble, flip it over and check the colour on the other side. Repeat until the batter turns golden brown. The pan should be at the correct temperature for making the dorayaki.

5. Pour a tablespoonful of batter into the frying pan, ensuring that the shape is regular and round. When the batter starts to bubble, flip the pancake over. Cook for about 30 seconds, then remove from the frying pan. Place the pancake lighter side up on a wire rack to cool. Repeat until the batter is used up.

6. Sandwich a portion of *koshi-an* between two pancakes to form a *dorayaki*. Serve.

7. *Dorayaki* can be stored in the freezer for up to 3 days. Thaw in the chiller for 3–4 hours before serving, or warm in a toaster oven.

WARABI MOCHI
(MOCHI COATED WITH SOY BEAN POWDER)

—————— makes about 4 servings ——————

Kinako (soy bean powder) 20 g

Icing sugar 20 g

Salt a pinch

Warabi mochi flour 80 g

Water 280 ml

1. Place the *kinako*, icing sugar and salt in a small bowl. Mix well and set aside for dusting the mochi.

2. Prepare the mochi. Place the *warabi* mochi flour and water in a saucepan and mix well with a rubber spatula.

3. Place the saucepan over medium heat and stir until the mixture thickens.

4. Lower the heat and continue stirring until the mixture is translucent. Remove from heat.

5. Wet a small metal tray with water. Transfer the mochi mixture to the tray and cover with plastic wrap. Place into a larger tray filled with iced water and set aside to cool and harden.

6. Cut the mochi into bite-size pieces. Dust with *kinako* mixture and serve immediately.

MITARASHI DANGO
(GRILLED DUMPLINGS WITH SOY SAUCE GLAZE)

—— makes 4 sticks ——

Bamboo skewers 4
***Shiratama* flour** 100 g
Lukewarm water (50°C) 70 ml

SOY SAUCE GLAZE
Light soy sauce 15 ml
Mirin 15 ml
Japanese custard sugar 40 g
Cornflour 7 g
Water 90 ml

1. Soak 4 bamboo skewers in water. Set aside until needed.

2. Prepare the soy sauce glaze. Place all the ingredients for the glaze in a small pot and mix well. Cook over low heat, stirring until the mixture thickens. Transfer to a small bowl.

3. Prepare the *dango*. In a microwave-safe bowl, stir the *shiratama* flour and sugar into the lukewarm water until the mixture is smooth. Cover the bowl and cook in a microwave oven on High for about 3 minutes. Stir the mixture to ensure that the heat is distributed evenly. Repeat to cook for another 2 minutes, then stir the mixture until it is smooth and no longer sticky. If the mixture is still sticky, cook for another minute and stir again.

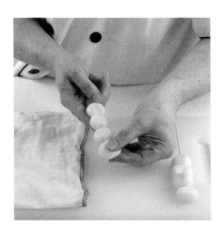

4. Transfer the mixture onto a clean dishcloth. Divide the mixture into 2 equal portions and roll each portion into a rod. Cut each rod into 8 equal pieces and thread 4 pieces into each bamboo skewer.

5. Place a wire mesh over an open flame on the stovetop and grill the skewered *dango* to char it slightly.

6. Brush the *dango* with the glaze and serve.

7. The *dango* can be wrapped and stored in an airtight container in the freezer after step 4. It will keep for up to 1 week. Grill before serving.

KUSA MOCHI
(JAPANESE MUGWORT MOCHI)

— makes 6 pieces —

Canola oil as needed

Tsubu-an **(page 20)** 100 g

Mochi flour 125 g

Japanese custard sugar 10 g, sifted

Dried *yomogi* **(Japanese mugwort)** 2 Tbsp

Lukewarm water (50°C) 140 ml

Potato starch as needed

Kinako **(soy bean powder)** 10 g

1. Prepare a 30-cm square sheet of baking paper. Brush with canola oil and set aside.

2. Divide the *tsubu-an* into 6 equal portions and roll into balls. Cover and set aside.

3. Soak the dried *yomogi* in a bowl of warm water to soften. Drain and mash with a fork.

4. To make the *kusa-mochi*, combine the mochi flour, sifted sugar and mashed dried *yomogi* in a mixing bowl. Add the lukewarm water and mix well.

Tip Wet your hands before shaping the mochi to prevent it from sticking to your hands.

5. Cover the bowl with plastic wrap and cook in a microwave oven on Medium for 1 minute. Stir the mixture, then cover the bowl and cook for another 1 minute 30 seconds. Repeat this process of cooking and stirring until the mixture is smooth and elastic.

6. Place the mixture on the prepared baking paper and use the paper to bring the mixture together into a ball. Dust a work surface with potato starch and roll the mixture into a cylinder. Cut into 6 equal pieces.

7. Press and flatten a portion of mixture, then top with a ball of *tsubu-an*. Bring up the sides to enclose the *tsubu-an*. Repeat with the remaining ingredients.

8. Dust the bottom of each ball with *kinako*. Serve immediately.

DAIGAKU IMO
(HONEY-GLAZED SWEET POTATOES)

—— Makes 3–4 servings ——

Sweet potatoes 250 g
Canola oil 15 ml
Black sesame seeds ¼ tsp

SAUCE
Japanese custard sugar 30 g
Honey 20 g
Light soy sauce 7.5 ml
Water 30 ml
Canola oil 15 ml

1. Wash and scrub the sweet potatoes well as they will be cooked with the skin on. Cut into bite-size pieces.

2. Place the sweet potatoes on a microwave-safe plate and cook in a microwave oven on Medium-High for about 6 minutes. Test that the sweet potato is cooked by piercing with a bamboo skewer. The bamboo skewer should go through easily. Cook the sweet potato for another minute if necessary.

3. Heat the oil in a saucepan over medium heat. Add the sweet potatoes and cook until they start to brown. Transfer to a plate.

4. Place all the ingredients for the sauce in the saucepan and stir over low heat until well mixed and the sauce is a little sticky. Return the sweet potatoes to the pan. Mix to coat each piece well with the sauce.

5. Transfer to a plate and sprinkle with black sesame seeds. Serve.

6. *Daigaku-imo* can be stored in an airtight container in the refrigerator for up to 2 days. Reheat in a toaster oven before consuming.

KASUTERA
(HONEY CASTELLA)

— makes 12–14 small cakes —

Eggs 4, medium
Japanese custard sugar 100 g
Honey 120 g
Mirin 30 ml
Pastry flour 120 g, sifted
Canola oil 30 ml

1. Prepare 12–14 cake moulds, each about 12 x 6 x 3.5-cm. Line with paper cases.

2. Prepare 1–2 square baking trays large enough to hold the cake moulds. Line each tray with 3 layers of thick newsprint paper. Use a water spray to wet the paper. Set aside.

3. Preheat the oven to 180°C.

4. Crack the eggs into a heatproof mixing bowl and whisk. Add the sugar, honey and mirin and whisk again.

5. Place the mixing bowl into a larger bowl or pot filled with hot water. Place over low heat and whisk until the egg mixture is warm, about 37–40°C.

6.   Remove the mixing bowl from the hot water and whisk the mixture until it becomes whitish in colour.

7.   Add the pastry flour and whisk until just incorporated.

8.   Add the canola oil and mix until the batter is smooth. The batter should fall in ribbons when lifted with a spatula.

9.   Spoon the batter into the prepared moulds. Arrange on the baking trays and spray the batter lightly with water.

10. Bake for 5 minutes, then spray again lightly with water and bake for 15 minutes.

11. Lower the oven temperature to 160°C and bake for a further 15 minutes until the cakes are golden brown in colour.

12. Leave to cool before serving. The cakes will keep for 2–3 days.

KARINTOU
(DEEP-FRIED BLACK SUGAR STICKS)

—————————————— Makes 45–50 pieces ——————————————

Bread flour 75 g

Pastry flour 25 g

Salt ⅛ tsp

Japanese custard sugar 5 g

Baking powder ⅙ tsp

Water ⅙ tsp + 50 ml

Canola oil as needed

SYRUP

Japanese black sugar 60 g

Cornflour 7 g

Water 20 ml

1. Sift the bread flour, pastry flour, salt and sugar into a mixing bowl.

2. Mix the baking powder with ⅙ tsp water in a small bowl and add to the mixing bowl. Add another 50 ml water and knead to get a smooth dough. Cover with plastic wrap and refrigerate for about 30 minutes.

3. Dust a cutting board with some flour. Place the chilled dough on the cutting board and roll into a sheet about 0.3-cm thick. Cut into 5 x 0.3-cm sticks. Keep them slightly apart so they do not stick.

4. Heat sufficient oil for deep-frying in a pan until about 180°C. Gently lower the dough sticks into the hot oil and deep-fry for about 3 minutes or until golden brown. Remove and set aside to drain. Place in a mixing bowl.

5. Prepare the syrup. Mix the black sugar, cornflour and water in a microwave-safe bowl and cook in the microwave oven on High for about 20 seconds. Remove and stir well, then cook for another 30–40 seconds until the mixture starts to bubble and boil, and is sticky.

6. Pour the syrup over the fried dough sticks and mix well. Place the dough sticks on a sheet of baking paper for the syrup to set, keeping them slightly apart so they do not stick.

7. Serve or store in an airtight container for up to 3 days.

SATSUMA IMO KINTSUBA
(PAN-FRIED SWEET POTATO SQUARES)

— makes 20 pieces —

Sweet potatoes 500 g

Water 200 ml

Agar-agar strips 5 g

Japanese custard sugar 100 g

Black sesame seeds ½ tsp

COATING

Pastry flour 50 g

Shiratama **flour** 1 Tbsp, finely pounded

Ground cinnamon 1 tsp

Japanese custard sugar ½ tsp

Salt a pinch

Water 120 ml

1. Rinse the sweet potatoes so they are wet, then wrap in two layers of aluminium foil. Cook in the toaster oven for about 50 minutes, or until tender.

2. Unwrap and peel the sweet potatoes. Dice and place into a food processor. Blend into a smooth purée.

3. Fill a pan with 200 ml water and sprinkle with the gelatin powder. Place the pan over medium heat and mix until the gelatin powder is dissolved. Add 100 g sugar and stir until the sugar is dissolved. Add the sweet potato purée and mix well.

4. Transfer the sweet potato mixture to the lined aluminium tray. Refrigerate for about 30 minutes for the mixture to set.

5. Prepare the coating. In a mixing bowl, mix the pastry flour, *shiratama* flour, cinnamon and sugar. Add half the water and whisk, then add the remaining water and whisk again. Pour through a sieve to remove any lumps.

6. Remove the set sweet potato mixture from the refrigerator and cut into 20 square pieces.

7. Heat a frying pan over low heat. Dip one side of a sweet potato square into the coating and place into the pan, coating side down. It will take 5–10 seconds to cook the coating and it should stick to the sweet potato square. Cook for another 5–10 seconds if it doesn't. Repeat to coat and cook each side. Do this in batches depending on the size of your pan.

8. Let cool before serving. Garnish with black sesame seeds. Consume within the day.

MIZUYOUKAN
(SWEET RED BEAN PASTE JELLY)

———————————————— Makes one 20-cm tray ————————————————

Agar-agar strips 4 g

Water 500 ml + 40 ml

Japanese custard sugar 200 g

Koshi-an **(page 22)** 300 g

Kuzu **powder** 5 g

Salt a pinch

1. Soak the agar-agar strips in water overnight. Line a 20-cm square tray with baking paper.

2. Drain the agar-agar strips and place in a small pan. Add 500 ml water and place over high heat. Bring the water to the boil and stir to dissolve the agar-agar. When the agar-agar is dissolved, stir in the sugar.

3. Pour the contents of the pan through a strainer into a bowl, then return the mixture to the pan. Place over medium heat and add the *koshi-an*. Stir until the koshi-an dissolves and the mixture comes to a boil. Remove from heat.

4. In a bowl, mix the *kuzu* powder with 40 ml water. Stir until the *kuzu* is dissolved. Add 180 ml of the *koshi-an* mixture and mix well.

5. Pour the *kuzu-koshi-an* mixture into the pan and bring to the boil over medium heat, stirring well with a spatula. Let boil for 3 minutes, stirring all the while. Remove from heat and stir in the salt.

6. Fill a large heatproof bowl with iced water. Place the pan in the water and stir the mixture slowly to cool it. As the mixture cools, it will become sticky.

7. Pour the mixture into the prepared tray. Cover and leave to set. When set, refrigerate for about 30 minutes. Cut and serve, or store refrigerated for up to 2 days.

ICHIGO DAIFUKU
(STRAWBERRY RED BEAN MOCHI)

— Makes 6 pieces —

Strawberries 6

Tsubu-an **(page 20)** 120 g

Potato starch 15 g

Shiratama **flour** 60 g

Water 60 ml + 60 ml

Japanese custard sugar 40 g, sifted

Glucose ½ tsp

1. Rinse and hull the strawberries, then pat them dry.

2. Divide the *tsubu-an* into 6 equal portions.

3. Roll a portion of *tsubu-an* into a ball and flatten slightly. Place a strawberry in the centre and bring the *tsubu-an* up to enclose the strawberry. Roll between your palms to form a round. Repeat with the remaining ingredients. Keep covered.

4. Sprinkle an aluminium tray with some potato starch. Set aside.

5. In a glass bowl, mix the *shiratama* flour with 60 ml water. Stir with a wooden spatula until well mixed. Add another 60 ml water and continue to stir. Add the Japanese custard sugar and mix well.

6. Place the *shiratama* mixture in the microwave oven and cook for 1 minute on Medium. Remove and mix, then repeat to cook and mix the mixture another two times. The resulting dough should be translucent and shiny. Use a spatula to mix the dough until it is sticky.

7. Add glucose and stir well.

8. Transfer the dough to the prepared aluminium tray and fold in half. Be careful not to get any potato starch on the top surface of the dough or it will not stick when folded.

9. Cut the dough into 6 equal portions. Shape each portion into a round and flatten slightly. Remove any potato starch on your hands with a brush.

10. Place a wrapped strawberry in the middle of a dough round with the tip of the strawberry facing down. Bring the edges of the dough up around the wrapped strawberry and enclose. Place the *ichigo daifuku* on a serving plate with the strawberry tip facing upwards. Repeat with the remaining ingredients.

11. Serve immediately.

MODERN WAGASHI

TOMATO NO KUZU MANJU
(KUZU JELLY WITH TOMATO)

— Makes 5 pieces —

KUZU MANJU

Kuzu **powder** 30 g

Water 150 ml

Japanese custard sugar 60 g

SWEETENED TOMATOES

Cherry tomatoes 5

Water 80 ml

Japanese custard sugar 40 g

> **Note** Do not refrigerate the dumplings for more than 30 minutes as they will harden and not be edible.

1. Prepare the sweetened tomatoes. Cut an X on the top of each tomato. Fill a bowl with iced water. Bring some water to the boil in a pan and blanch the tomatoes for 30 seconds. Remove with a strainer and plunge immediately into iced water to cool. Peel the tomatoes and set aside.

2. In a microwave-safe bowl, heat the water and sugar on Medium-High for 1 minute 30 seconds. Place the peeled tomatoes into the syrup and leave to soak.

3. Prepare the *kuzu manju*. Place the *kuzu* powder in a small saucepan and gradually add the water, whisking until the powder is dissolved and the mixture is smooth. Add the sugar and mix well. Place the pan over medium heat, stirring constantly until the mixture starts to thicken. Remove from heat and continue mixing until the mixture is translucent.

4. Line a small diameter bowl with plastic wrap. Place about one-fifth of the *kuzu* mixture into the bowl and add a tomato. Bring the edges of the plastic wrap up to enclose the mixture. Secure with a wire tie. Repeat with the rest of the ingredients.

5. Line a steamer with baking paper and arrange the dumplings in the steamer. Steam over high heat for about 10 minutes or until the mixture is translucent. Refrigerate the dumplings for 30 minutes.

6. Unwrap and serve immediately.

CINNAMON NAMA YATSUHASHI
(CINNAMON-FLAVOURED MOCHI)

—————————— Makes 9 pieces ——————————

Mochi flour 40 g

Water 60 ml

Shiratama **flour** 20 g

Japanese custard sugar 70 g

Ground cinnamon 2 tsp

> **Tip** If you find it hard to cut the *nama-yatsuhashi* with a knife, use a pair of kitchen scissors. Whether using a knife or a pair of scissors, ensure that they are dry.

1. Line a glass tray with baking paper. Set aside.

2. Place the mochi flour in a mixing bowl. Gradually add the water, mixing with a rubber spatula until the mixture is smooth. Add the shiratama flour and sugar and mix well.

3. Place the mixture on the prepared glass tray and steam for about 15 minutes.

4. Remove the glass tray from the steamer. Fold the baking paper inwards to flatten the mixture. Set aside to cool. When cool, peel off the baking paper.

5. Sprinkle a clean cutting board with some ground cinnamon. Place the cooled mixture on the cutting board and sprinkle with the remaining cinnamon. Knead the mixture with the cinnamon until it is no longer sticky.

6. Roll it out into a thin sheet about 18 x 18-cm.

7. Cut into 6-cm squares and serve immediately.

SATSUMAIMO TO RINGO NO CHAKIN
(SWEET POTATO & APPLE CHAKIN)

───────── Makes 16–18 pieces ─────────

Sweet potatoes 300 g

Salt a pinch

Apple 100 g

Japanese custard sugar 20 g

Mixed fruit 30 g

Fresh cream 30 ml

1. Peel the sweet potatoes and cut into 2-cm cubes. Wrap in aluminium foil and cook in the toaster oven for about 30 minutes, or until tender.

2. Place the sweet potatoes in a mixing bowl. Mash while still warm. Season with salt and set aside to cool.

3. Core the apple and slice thinly. Place in a pan over low heat. Add sugar and cook, stirring, for 15 minutes.

4. Add the cooked apple to the sweet potato mash. Mix well.

5. Mix the mixed fruit with the cream. Add to the sweet potato mash and mix again.

> **Tip** The mixed fruit adds colour to the dumplings. Use only red or green glacé cherries or raisins to adjust the colour as desired. Vary it according to the colour theme of your party!

6. Line a small bowl with plastic wrap and spoon in 20 g of the sweet potato mixture.

7. Twist the plastic wrap and shape the mixture into a tight dumpling.

8. Repeat to make more dumplings until the mash is used up. Refrigerate for about 30 minutes.

9. Unwrap the dumplings and arrange on a serving plate. Serve immediately or store in an airtight container for up to 2 days.

BERRY KUZU
(KUZU JELLY WITH BERRIES & CITRUS PEEL)

— Makes 8–10 servings —

ORANGE PEEL MIXTURE

Orange peel 40 g

Orange liqueur 10 ml

White wine 10 ml

SHIRO-AN MIXTURE

Shiro-an **(page 18)** 100 g

Water 50 ml + 450 ml

Kuzu **powder** 50 g

Japanese custard sugar 100 g

Glucose 20 g

Raspberries 70 g

Orange liqueur 5 ml

Mint leaves 8–10 sprigs

1. Prepare the orange peel mixture. Mix the orange peel, orange liqueur and white wine in a bowl. Let sit for about an hour.

2. Prepare the *shiro-an* mixture. Mix the shiro-an with 50 ml water in a medium bowl. Set aside.

3. Place the *kuzu* powder in a pan over medium heat. Gradually add 450 ml water, stirring all the while.

4. Add sugar and glucose and continue to stir, ensuring that the mixture does not stick to the bottom of the pan. When the mixture starts to become sticky, remove from heat.

5. Take a scoop of the *kuzu* mixture and add to the bowl of *shiro-an*. Mix well and set aside.

6. Return the saucepan to medium heat and continue to stir until the mixture is translucent. Remove from heat.

7. Pour the *kuzu* mixture into the shiro-an mixture and mix well for 1–2 minutes. Set aside to cool for 4–5 minutes.

8. Add the orange peel mixture, raspberries and orange liqueur.

9. Divide the mixture among 8–10 serving cups. Let cool before refrigerating for about 30 minutes to set and chill. Garnish and serve.

10. This jelly can be kept refrigerated for up to 2 days.

ICHIGO MILKY SHIRATAMA
(MILKY STRAWBERRY MOCHI)

— Makes 16 pieces —

Strawberries 120 g or more as needed

Shiratama **flour** 70 g

Sweetened condensed milk 50 g

Koshi-an **(page 22)** 80 g

Tip As the moisture content of strawberries vary, add the strawberries a little at a time and knead until the dough is soft. The texture of the dough should be soft like a ear lobe.

You can also experiment using other fruit to make the *shiratama*.

---

1. Rinse and hull the strawberries, then pat them dry. Cut into small cubes and place in a bowl. Add the *shiratama* flour and knead to get a soft dough. The mixture should not stick to your hands.

2. Roll the dough into a long cylinder and cut into two equal lengths. Place them side by side, then cut into 8 pieces per length. Roll each portion into a ball, then flatten slightly.

3. Prepare a bowl of iced water and set aside.

4. Boil a pot of water and lower the strawberry *shiratama* balls in to cook. After 1–2 minutes, the balls should float. Let cook for another 10 seconds, then scoop the balls out and place into the bowl of iced water to cool.

5. Drain the balls and place into serving bowls. Drizzle with condensed milk and top with some *koshi-an*. Serve.

6. The *shiratama* balls can be covered with plastic wrap and kept in the freezer for up to 1 week. Thaw in the chiller for 3–4 hours before topping with condensed milk and *koshi-an*.

EDAMAME TOFU DANGO
(TOFU DUMPLINGS WITH EDAMAME TOPPING)

--- Makes 8 pieces ---

Frozen unsalted edamame 200 g

Japanese custard sugar 30 g

Fresh cream 30 ml

Salt a pinch

Black sesame seeds 1 tsp

TOFU DANGO

Shiratama **flour** 80 g

Silken tofu 80 g

Japanese custard sugar 30 g + 5 g

> **Note** In this recipe, edamame beans are used in a similar way to red beans and butter beans to produce a creamy, sweet bean paste. Try it! You will be surprised at how good it tastes!

1. Boil a pot of water and cook the edamame for 4–5 minutes. Strain the edamame and let cool slightly, then remove the beans from the pods. Squeeze the beans out of their skins and discard the skins.

2. While the beans are still warm, place them in a food processor and blend into a paste. Transfer to a bowl. Add the sugar, cream and salt and mix well. Set aside.

3. Prepare the tofu *dango*. In another bowl, mix the *shiratama* flour, silken tofu and sugar. Knead into a soft dough. If the mixture feels dry, add a little water and knead until the dough is soft and pliable.

4. Divide the dough into 8 equal portions and roll each portion into a ball. Flatten the centre of the balls slightly by pressing between your thumb and index finger.

5. Prepare a bowl of iced water and set aside.

6. Boil a pot of water and lower the *shiratama* balls in to cook. After 2–3 minutes, the balls should float. Let cook for another 10 seconds, then scoop the balls out and place into the bowl of iced water to cool.

7. Drain the balls and pat dry with a clean kitchen towel. Place balls into individual serving bowls and top with some edamame paste. Garnish with black sesame seeds and serve immediately.

BANANA GURATAN
(BANANA GRATIN)

—————————————— Makes two 12-cm puddings ——————————————

Eggs 2, medium

Japanese custard sugar 20 g

Pastry flour 12 g

Milk 180 ml

Ripe bananas 2, each about 150 g

Koshi-an **(page 22)** 50 g

1. Prepare the batter. Crack the eggs into a mixing bowl and stir with a whisk. Add the sugar and pastry flour and mix well.

2. Add the milk and stir well. Strain the mixture to remove any lumps. Set aside.

3. Peel the bananas and cut into 2-cm thick slices.

4. Arrange the bananas in two 12-cm round gratin dishes and pour over half the batter. Dot with the *koshi-an*, then pour over the remaining batter.

5. Place the gratin dishes in an oven toaster and cook for about 10 minutes, or until the surface is golden brown. Remove and serve immediately.

AZUKI PANNAKOTTA
(RED BEAN PANNA COTTA)

———Makes 4–5 servings———

Leaf gelatin 5 g

Milk 150 ml

Japanese custard sugar 20 g

Koshi-an **(page 22)** 80 g

Fresh cream 100 ml

1. Place the leaf gelatin in a bowl of iced water to soften. Set aside.

2. Pour the milk into a pan and heat to 70°C.

3. Remove the gelatin from the iced water and squeeze out the excess water. Add to the heated milk. Add the sugar and mix until both the sugar and gelatin are dissolved and the milk is cool.

4. Stir in the *koshi-an* and cream.

5. Pour the mixture into 4–5 small moulds and refrigerate for 30 minutes.

6. Unmould the panna cotta and serve.

7. If not serving immediately, leave the panna cotta in the moulds and store refrigerated for up to 2 days.

HOUJICHA-ANNIN
(ROASTED GREEN TEA PUDDING)

— Makes 2 servings —

Leaf gelatin 4 g

Water 100 ml

Japanese custard sugar 23 g

Chinese almond powder 23 g

Milk 150 ml

Fresh cream 50 ml

Fresh and/or dried fruit
as desired

HOUJI SYRUP

Water 85 ml

Japanese custard sugar 13 g

Houjicha 1.5 g

> **Tip** The jelly can also be set in small moulds and served on plates with the *houji* syrup drizzled over.

1. Place the leaf gelatin in a bowl of iced water to soften. Set aside.

2. Place the water, sugar and Chinese almond powder in a pan over medium heat. Stir with a spatula until the sugar is melted and the mixture is smooth.

3. Remove the gelatin from the iced water and squeeze out the excess water. Add to the pan.

4. Mix the milk and cream in a bowl, then add to the pan. Stir until the gelatin is dissolved.

5. Strain the mixture and pour into 2 serving cups. Cover and refrigerate for 1 hour to set and chill.

6. In the meantime, prepare the *houji* syrup. Place the water and sugar in a pan and bring to the boil over low heat. When it starts to boil, remove from heat and add the *houjicha*. Let sit for 3 minutes. Strain the *houji* syrup and set aside to cool.

7. Top the jelly with fresh and/or dried fruits and drizzle with *houji* syrup. Serve.

8. *Houjicha-annin* can be kept refrigerated for up to 2 days.

NIHONSHU TO TOUNYU JELLY
(SAKE & SOY BEAN JELLY)

Makes 4 servings

SOY BEAN JELLY

Leaf gelatin 5 g

Fresh cream 25 ml

Milk 65 ml

Japanese custard sugar 25 g

Soy milk 125 ml

NIHONSHU JELLY

Leaf gelatin 8 g

Water 300 ml

Japanese custard sugar 55 g

Dry sake 125 ml

1. Prepare the soy bean jelly. Place the leaf gelatin in a bowl of iced water to soften. Set aside.

2. Place the cream, milk and sugar in a small saucepan over medium heat. Stir until the sugar is melted. Remove the gelatin from the iced water and squeeze out the excess water. Add to the pan. Add the soy milk and stir until the gelatin is dissolved.

3. Strain the mixture equally into 4 small glasses. Refrigerate for about 3 hours until the jelly is set.

4. Prepare the *nihonshu* jelly. Place the leaf gelatin in a bowl of iced water to soften. Set aside.

5. Place the water and sugar in a small saucepan over medium heat. Stir until the sugar is melted. Remove the gelatin from the iced water and squeeze out the excess water. Add to the pan. Add the sake and stir until the gelatin is dissolved.

6. Strain the mixture into an aluminium tray. Refrigerate for about 3 hours until the jelly is set.

7. To assemble, cut the *nihonshu* jelly into small cubes and spoon over the soy bean jelly. Serve.

8. The jelly can be kept refrigerated for up to 2 days.

KABUCHA PUDDING
(PUMPKIN PUDDING)

— Makes 6 small puddings —

Pumpkin 280 g

Eggs 3, medium

Japanese custard sugar 80 g

Fresh cream 200 ml

Milk 300 ml

CARAMEL

Water 20 ml

Japanese custard sugar 160 g

Hot water 20 ml

1. Preheat the oven to 170°C. Prepare 6 ramekins, each about 7.5-cm wide.

2. Prepare the caramel. Place the water and sugar in a small saucepan over medium heat. Stir constantly with a wooden spatula until the mixture is golden brown. Add the hot water gradually while stirring until well-mixed.

3. Spoon 1 tsp of the warm caramel into each ramekin. Place on a roasting pan and set aside.

4. Cut the pumpkin into 8 even pieces with the skin on. Place the pumpkin in the microwave oven and cook on High for about 5 minutes until the pumpkin is tender.

5. Peel the pumpkin and place in a food processor with the eggs, sugar, cream and half the milk. Process until smooth. Pour the pumpkin mixture into a glass bowl.

6. In a small saucepan, heat the remaining 150 ml milk to about 65°C. Add to the pumpkin mixture and mix well.

7. Ladle the pumpkin mixture into the prepared ramekins. Fill the roasting pan with hot water to come halfway up the sides of ramekins. Bake for 30–35 minutes until pudding is set. Serve immediately.

YUKIDAMA COOKIES
(SNOWBALL COOKIES)

Makes 18–20 small cookies

Unsalted butter 60 g

Pastry flour 100 g, sifted

Japanese custard sugar 20 g

Walnuts 20 g, finely chopped

Japanese custard sugar 30 g

Kinako **(soy bean powder)** 30 g

1. Place a small saucepan over low heat. Add the butter and let it melt. Pour into a glass mixing bowl. Add the flour, sugar and walnuts and mix well into a dough.

2. Roll the dough into a long cylinder about 2-cm in diameter. Cut into two equal lengths. Cut each length into 8–10 pieces. Roll each piece into a ball.

3. Place the balls on a lined baking tray. Cover and set aside in the freezer for about 30 minutes.

4. Preheat the oven to 170°C and bake the cookies for 15 minutes. Set aside to cool.

5. Mix the icing sugar with the *kinako* and dust the cookies before serving.

TOFU YUZU-CHA MAFIN
(TOFU YUZU-CHA MUFFINS)

—— Makes about 8 muffins ——

Pastry flour 125 g

Baking powder 5 g

Butter 60 g

Silken tofu 200 g

Japanese black sugar 60 g

Walnuts 40 g, finely chopped

Yuzu-cha 40 g

1. Preheat the oven to 180°C. Line 8 muffin cups with paper liners.

2. Sift the pastry flour and baking powder into a mixing bowl. Set aside.

3. Place a pan over low heat. Add the butter and let it melt.

4. Place the tofu, black sugar and melted butter into a food processor and process until smooth. Transfer to a mixing bowl.

5. Add the walnuts and *yuzu-cha* to the tofu mixture. Mix well with a spatula.

6. Add the sifted flour mixture and mix until just incorporated.

7. Spoon the mixture into the prepared muffin cups and bake for 20 minutes or until a skewer inserted into the centre of cakes comes out clean.

8. Set aside to cool before serving.

MATCHA TOFU PUDDING
(MATCHA TOFU PUDDING)

Makes 4 servings

Leaf gelatin 6 g

Cream cheese 80 g,
  at room temperature

Silken tofu 150 g

Sweetened condensed milk 30 g

Japanese custard sugar 20 g

Lemon juice 10 ml

Unsalted butter 10 g

Milk 50 ml

TOPPING

Matcha powder as needed

Koshi-an **(page 22)** as needed

Fresh fruit as desired

> **Tip** Set this dessert in
> a casserole dish for a
> different presentation.

1. Place the leaf gelatin in a bowl of iced water to soften. Set aside.

2. Place the cream cheese in a glass mixing bowl and stir with a whisk until smooth. Add the tofu and mix well. Add the condensed milk, sugar and lemon juice and mix again. Set aside.

3. Place the butter and milk in a pan over medium heat and stir until the butter is melted.

4. Remove the gelatin from the iced water and squeeze out the excess water. Add the gelatin to the pan and stir. Pour contents of the pan into the cream cheese mixture and mix well.

5. Pour the mixture into 4 serving cups, cover and refrigerate for about 2 hours to set and chill.

6. Dust with matcha powder and top with *koshi-an*. Garnish wilth fresh fruit before serving.

7. The jelly can be kept refrigerated for up to 2 days.

KABOCHA FINANSHE
(PUMPKIN FINANCIERS)

—————————————— Makes 10–12 small cakes ——————————————

Pastry flour 20 g

Baking powder 2 g

Ground cinnamon 2 g

Almond powder 20 g

Unsalted butter 100 g

Pumpkin 80 g

Japanese black sugar 40 g

Egg whites 90 g

> **Tip** The pumpkin need not be peeled as the skin is edible. Mash it together with the yellow flesh.

1. Preheat the oven to 200°C. Prepare a financier mould.

2. Sift the pastry flour, baking powder and cinnamon into a mixing bowl. Add the almond powder and mix well. Set aside.

3. Place a pan over low heat. Add the butter and let it melt. Set aside.

4. Cut the pumpkin into small cubes. Place in a microwave-safe bowl and cook in the microwave oven on High for 3–5 minutes, or until tender.

5. Mash the pumpkin while warm. Add the black sugar and mix well with a whisk.

6. Add the egg whites gradually and mix well.

7. Add the flour mixture and mix to incorporate.

8. Add the melted butter and mix again.

9. Spoon the batter into the prepared financier mould and bake for about 17 minutes or until cakes are risen and golden. Set aside to cool before serving.

KUZU KIRI
(KUZU JELLY STRIPS WITH UME SAUCE)

--- Makes about 5 servings ---

Kuzu powder 100 g
Water 300 ml
Marmalade as needed

UME SAUCE

Water 200 ml
Japanese black sugar 50 g
Umeshu 45 g

1. Prepare the *ume* sauce. Place the water and black sugar in a pan and bring to the boil. When the water starts to boil, add the *umeshu*. Remove from heat and set aside until needed.

2. Prepare a 20-cm square metal tray and a larger roasting pan. The metal tray should be able to sit inside the roasting pan. Fill the roasting pan with just enough water to come halfway up the side of the metal tray. Bring the water to the boil.

3. Place the *kuzu* powder in a mixing bowl. Add the water gradually while stirring. Mix well.

4. Pour the mixture into the prepared metal tray sitting in the roasting pan of water. Heat until the mixture is set.

5. Using metal tongs, carefully push the metal tray into the hot water to submerge it.

6. Let cook until the mixture is translucent.

7. Remove the tray and place it into a pan of iced water to cool the kuzu-kiri.

8. When cool, slice the *kuzu-kiri* into strips. Spoon into serving bowls and top with some marmalade. Drizzle with *ume* sauce and serve.

FU BROWNIE
(GLUTEN BROWNIE)

Makes one 18-cm round cake

Gluten cakes 45 g

Milk 200 ml

Mixed fruit 20 g

Honey 30 g

Unsalted butter 40 g,
    at room temperature

Japanese custard sugar 50 g + 20 g

Egg yolks 100 g

Egg whites 200 g

Pastry flour 70 g, sifted

Cocoa powder 45 g

1. Preheat the oven to 160°C. Line a 18-cm round baking tin with baking paper.

2. Place the gluten cakes and milk in a bowl. Mix well. Add mixed fruit and honey and mix again. Set aside.

3. Whisk the butter and 50 g sugar in a mixing bowl until the mixture is pale.

4. Add the egg yolks one at a time, whisking well after each addition.

5. Add the gluten mixture and mix well.

6. In a clean, grease-free bowl, beat the egg whites with 20 g sugar until soft peaks form.

7. Add half the beaten egg whites to the egg yolk mixture and mix well. Add the flour and cocoa powder and mix well.

8. Add the remainder of the beaten egg whites and mix well.

9. Spoon the batter into the prepared baking tin. Bake for 30 minutes or until a skewer inserted into the centre of cake comes out clean.

10. Set aside to cool before slicing to serve. Store in a cool, dry place for up to 2 days.

PACKAGING IDEAS

Wagashi makes an ideal gift whatever the occasion. Here are some ideas to personalise your *wagashi* to make them extra special!

Place the *wagashi* in a pretty container and/or wrap with food-grade plastic. Decorate with ribbons and a gift tag.

Place the *wagashi* in a mug or a jar which can be kept long after the *wagashi* has been eaten.

To present a variety of *wagashi*, place them in paper cupcake cases in a pretty box, then attach a fork to complete the gift!

PAIRING WAGASHI WITH DRINKS

Wagashi is best enjoyed with a drink. Here are some recommendations for pairing beverages with the *wagashi* featured in this book.

DORAYAKI PAGE 27 + GYOKURO

WARABI-MOCHI PAGE 28 + SENCHA

MITARASHI DANGO PAGE 30 + SENCHA

KUSA-MOCHI PAGE 34 + HOUJICHA

DAIGAKU-IMO PAGE 38 + GYOKURO

KASUTERA PAGE 40 + COFFEE

KARINTOU PAGE 44   +   HOUJICHA

 +     +

SATSUMA IMO KINTSUBA PAGE 46   SAKURA CHA   MIZUYOUKAN PAGE 50   GYOKURO

 +     +

ICHIGO DAIFUKU PAGE 52   SENCHA   TOMATO NO KUZU MANJU PAGE 58   ENGLISH BREAKFAST TEA

 +     +

CINNAMON NAMA-YATSUHASHI PAGE 60   MATCHA   SATSUMAIMO TO RINGO NO CHAKIN PAGE 62   EARL GREY

BERRY KUZU
PAGE 66

+

LEMON TEA

ICHIGO MIRUKII
SHIRATAMA PAGE 71

+

HOUJICHA

EDAMAME TOFU
DANGO PAGE 72

+

SENCHA

BANANA
GURATAN PAGE 75

+

ENGLISH
BREAKFAST TEA

AZUKI
PANNAKOTTA PAGE 76

+

MATCHA

HOUJICHA-ANNIN
PAGE 78

+

ENGLISH
BREAKFAST TEA

NIHONSHU TO
TOUNYU JELLY
PAGE 80

+

GYOKURO

KABUCHA PUDDING PAGE 83 + EARL GREY

YUKIDAMA COOKIES PAGE 84 + COFFEE

TOFU YUZU-CHA MAFIN PAGE 86 + HOUJICHA

MATCHA TOFU PUDDING PAGE 88 + COFFEE

KABOCHA FINANSHE PAGE 90 + EARL GREY

KUZU-KIRI PAGE 92 + MATCHA

FU BROWNIE PAGE 96 + EARL GREY

GLOSSARY

The ingredients used in these recipes are available from Japanese supermarkets and some baking supply stores. They are photographed in their packaging to make it easier to identify them on the supermarket shelves, and any brand of the same ingredient will be suitable for use in these recipes.

Mochi Flour

Also known as *mochiko*, mochi flour is milled from a Japanese short grain glutinous rice, *mochigome*. It is popularly used in making Japanese *wagashi* such as mochi and *dango*, and also as a thickening agent in cooking. It is different from Asian glutinous rice flour and the latter should not be used as a substitute for mochi flour.

Kuzu Powder

Also known as *kuzu* starch or *kuzu* root powder, this superior starch is derived from the root of the *kuzu* plant. It is used as a thickening agent in stews and gravies, and also in making Japanese *wagashi*. It gives Japanese sweets such as *kuzu kiri* its translucent quality and firmess.

Warabi Mochi Flour

Also known as *warabiko*, this flour is used for making *warabi* mochi. Traditionally, *warabi* mochi is made using *hon warabiko* which is pure bracken starch, but as the starch is expensive and requires some skill to use, *warabi* mochi is now commonly made using *warabi* mochi flour which is a mixture of bracken starch, sweet potato flour and tapioca flour. This composition makes *warabi* mochi flour easy to handle for home cooks.

Shiratama Flour

Like mochi flour, *shiratama* flour is milled from *mochigome*, but it goes through a different process of soaking and grinding, and is sold as granules rather than powder. *Shiratama* flour produces *wagashi* that has a more refined texture than mochi flour.

Japanese Black Sugar
Also known as *kurozatou*, this pure cane sugar originates from Okinawa. It is rich in minerals and vitamins and has a complex molasses flavour that is salty, bitter and sweet. It is available as irregularly shaped pieces and in powder form.

Japanese Custard Sugar
Also known as *johakutou*, this white cane sugar is popularly used in Japanese baking and in making *wagashi*. It is a very fine, soft sugar, and it is used to give a moist sweetness to Japanese sweets. Castor sugar can be used as a substitute, but the final product with not be as moist.

Liquid Glucose
This clear, thick syrup is often used to give baked goods a soft texture and to add volume. It also helps baked goods retain moisture and freshness.

Yuzu-cha
Made from yuzu and honey, *yuzu-cha* is available in jars from supermarkets. It is sold as a tea to be diluted in water, but it can also be used in baking to add an exquisite and aromatic flavour to cakes and cookies.

Matcha Powder
This fine, powdered tea is used in the traditional Japanese tea ceremony, and is now also popularly used as an ingredient in baking and making other confections.

Houjicha Powder
Houjicha is a roasted green tea with a warm, sweet and smoky flavour. The ground form of the tea can be used to make a quick drink as well as to flavour cakes and other desserts.

Kinako
This fragrant, nutty-tasting powder is made from roasted soy beans. It is often used as a coating for *wagashi*, and is increasingly also used to flavour other confections such as cookies and ice cream.

Dried Yomogi
Yomogi or Japanese mugwort is used to add flavour, aroma and colour to mochi. Due to its anti-inflammatory properties, it is also consumed as a health food. It is available from Japanese supermarkets and health food stores.

Butter Beans

These large, cream-coloured beans have a delicate buttery flavour. Canned butter beans are a convenient option for making *shiro-an*, although the beans should be drained and soaked to remove some of the saltiness from the brine.

Azuki

Azuki beans can be red, green, yellow or white, but the name is now most commonly associated with the red beans. Azuki beans can be used in both sweet and savoury preparations, but they are mainly enjoyed in desserts.

Gluten Cakes

These gluten cakes are known as *fu* in Japanese. They are made by rinsing the starch out from wheat dough, then steaming and drying. It is a meat substitute in Zen cooking and is also enjoyed in Japanese soups and stews.

Sake

A Japanese wine made from fermented rice, sake or *nihonshu* can be enjoyed as a drink and also used in cooking and making desserts. The bottle shown here is my favourite brand of sake, produced in my hometown, Nara, the historical centre of sake production. It is light, with just a touch of sweetness and dryness, and has full flavour and character.

WEIGHTS & MEASURES

Quantities for this book are given in Metric and American (spoon and cup) measures. Standard spoon and cup measurements used are: 1 teaspoon = 5 ml, 1 tablespoon = 15 ml and 1 cup = 250 ml. All measures are level unless otherwise stated.

LIQUID AND VOLUME MEASURES

Metric	Imperial	American
5 ml	$1/6$ fl oz	1 teaspoon
10 ml	$1/3$ fl oz	1 dessertspoon
15 ml	$1/2$ fl oz	1 tablespoon
60 ml	2 fl oz	$1/4$ cup (4 tablespoons)
85 ml	$2^1/2$ fl oz	$1/3$ cup
90 ml	3 fl oz	$3/8$ cup (6 tablespoons)
125 ml	4 fl oz	$1/2$ cup
180 ml	6 fl oz	$3/4$ cup
250 ml	8 fl oz	1 cup
300 ml	10 fl oz ($1/2$ pint)	$1^1/4$ cups
375 ml	12 fl oz	$1^1/2$ cups
435 ml	14 fl oz	$1^3/4$ cups
500 ml	16 fl oz	2 cups
625 ml	20 fl oz (1 pint)	$2^1/2$ cups
750 ml	24 fl oz ($1^1/5$ pints)	3 cups
1 litre	32 fl oz ($1^3/5$ pints)	4 cups
1.25 litres	40 fl oz (2 pints)	5 cups
1.5 litres	48 fl oz ($2^2/5$ pints)	6 cups
2.5 litres	80 fl oz (4 pints)	10 cups

OVEN TEMPERATURE

	°C	°F	Gas Regulo
Very slow	120	250	1
Slow	150	300	2
Moderately slow	160	325	3
Moderate	180	350	4
Moderately hot	190/200	370/400	5/6
Hot	210/220	410/440	6/7
Very hot	230	450	8
Super hot	250/290	475/550	9/10

DRY MEASURES

Metric	Imperial
30 grams	1 ounce
45 grams	$1^1/2$ ounces
55 grams	2 ounces
70 grams	$2^1/2$ ounces
85 grams	3 ounces
100 grams	$3^1/2$ ounces
110 grams	4 ounces
125 grams	$4^1/2$ ounces
140 grams	5 ounces
280 grams	10 ounces
450 grams	16 ounces (1 pound)
500 grams	1 pound, $1^1/2$ ounces
700 grams	$1^1/2$ pounds
800 grams	$1^3/4$ pounds
1 kilogram	2 pounds, 3 ounces
1.5 kilograms	3 pounds, $4^1/2$ ounces
2 kilograms	4 pounds, 6 ounces

LENGTH

Metric	Imperial
0.5 cm	$1/4$ inch
1 cm	$1/2$ inch
1.5 cm	$3/4$ inch
2.5 cm	1 inch

ABBREVIATION

tsp	teaspoon
Tbsp	tablespoon
g	gram
kg	kilogram
ml	millilitre

THANK
YOU